Animals of the Night

SNAKES
AFTER DARK

Ruth O'Shaughnessy

Enslow Publishing
101 W. 23rd Street
Suite 240
New York, NY 10011
USA

enslow.com

Words to Know

camouflage—Coloring that helps something hide in its surroundings.

carnivore—An animal that eats meat.

constrict—To squeeze.

endangered—In danger of dying out.

Jacobson's organ—An organ in a snake that can sense some chemicals released by a nearby animal.

predator—An animal that eats other animals for food.

prey—An animal that is eaten by other animals.

venom—A poison made by an animal.

Contents

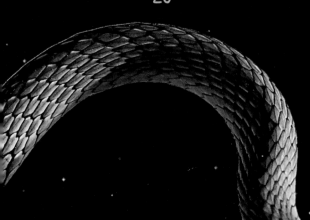

Dusk Falls

In the muggy warmth of a darkened rain forest, few creatures are moving. It is quiet, a time for most creatures to rest. But a large, hungry anaconda lies in wait.

Finally, a capybara passes by, and the snake grabs it, wrapping its long, scaly body around the giant rodent. A constrictor is not venomous. Rather, this type of snake uses the muscles in its body to **constrict**, or squeeze, its **prey** to death. Then the anaconda opens its mouth really wide, unhinging its jaw, and begins to swallow the capybara whole. Afterwards, the anaconda is full and won't need to eat again for a while.

Fun Fact!

A group of anacondas is called a bed or a knot.

A green anaconda is a large snake from the tropical rain forests of South America.

Slithering Serpents

Snakes are reptiles, like crocodiles, turtles, and lizards. A reptile's body temperature changes with its surroundings. On a cool day, a snake will rest in the sun to warm up. A snake that wants to cool down will crawl under a bush or a rock.

Nearly three thousand species, or types, of snakes are found in the world. Only some of them are venomous, or poisonous, though most snakes are not.

Snakes also come in all different sizes. The reticulated python can reach 45 feet (14 meters) long. That's the length of a bus! The green anaconda can weigh more than 400 pounds (181 kilograms) and can devour prey more than twice its size! The threadsnake is as small as a piece of spaghetti.

Fun Fact!

Scientists believe that snakes descended, or came from, lizards. Over time, they lost their limbs.

Pythons are among the largest snakes in the world.

Snakes do not have arms, legs, wings, or even ears. Scales cover their body. A snake's scales might look slimy, but they are really dry.

Although they don't have limbs, snakes do have skeletons. A snake's skeleton only has a skull and a long spine. Some snakes can twist themselves around objects. Many snakes can slip through narrow spaces or move into holes.

Fun Fact!

Snakes use their jawbones to hear.

These colorful scales belong to the Brazilian rainbow boa.

Snakes in Their Environment

Most snakes enjoy a warm climate. They can be found in fields and forests or on rocky hillsides. Cottonmouth snakes, also known as water moccasins, are mostly found in wetlands in the southeastern United States. Other big snakes live in grasslands and deserts. Rattlesnakes live in deserts and forests from Canada to South America, with many found in the United States.

And still other snakes live in trees, caves, or water. Many boa constrictors are good climbers. They are often spotted in rain forests. In some places, snakes are also found in towns and cities.

Cottonmouth snakes get their name from their white mouths. They are found in Kentucky, Tennessee, Virginia, Alabama, Georgia, and other southeastern states.

Many snakes use **camouflage**. This means that they blend into their environment. Brown or grayish rattlesnakes match the ground and rocks. Copperheads have wide reddish-brown bands to match logs and leaves in their surroundings.

Fun Fact!

Snakes are found on every continent except Antarctica.

A northern copperhead is camouflaged in a pile of dry leaves.

Snake Movement

Snakes move in several ways, even though they don't have legs, feet, or wings. One way they move is the S-shaped wave, which is used by many species of snake. The snake uses its muscles to curve its body. The curves of the snake's body push against the ground. This moves the snake forward in a wavy path.

Larger, heavier snakes use the belly crawl. They push down on their belly scales and slide forward. They move ahead in a nearly straight line.

Sidewinding is used by snakes that live in sandy environments, such as the sidewinder rattlesnake. To move forward, the snake lifts the main part of its body and thrusts it forward sideways. Then, it moves its head around and tail up to the rest of its body.

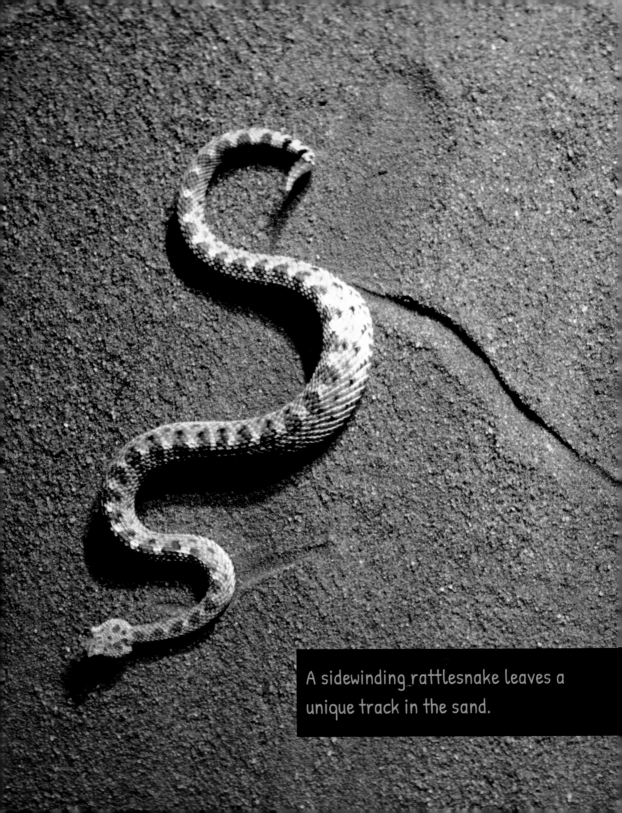

A sidewinding rattlesnake leaves a unique track in the sand.

How They Hunt

Snakes are **carnivores**, or meat eaters. They devour mice, rats, birds, frogs, turtles, rabbits, pigs, small deer, other snakes, and anything else that comes across their path. Big snakes eat big animals.

Many snakes are nocturnal. And most snakes are good night hunters. They do not have to use sight and hearing the way humans do. Instead, snakes use their other senses. A snake has a forked, or split, tongue. The snake flicks out its tongue, and when it goes back in its mouth, the tongue touches the snake's **Jacobson's organ**, which senses the taste and smell of a nearby animal. This lets the snake know that a meal is within reach.

Fun Fact!

A pit viper has pits, which are special organs, on each side of its head that sense the heat of prey.

A Mangrove cat snake flicks its tongue to find its prey.

Snakes also use nostrils to pick up stronger scents and those coming from far away. Snakes sometimes place their jaws on the ground to feel the other animals' movements as well.

Sometimes, snakes quietly sneak up on their prey. Other times, they wait for them. Often they will stay near an animal's trail. Prey is likely to pass there. They will wait in the same spot for days.

Venomous snakes like mambas and cobras use their deadly **venom** to kill the animals they eat. Constrictor snakes, such as boas and pythons, wrap their bodies around their prey and squeeze it to death.

A snake does not chew its food. It swallows its prey whole. The lower jaw of a snake's mouth opens very wide. A snake can eat animals that are larger than its head! The snake's strong jaw and throat muscles push the food into its stomach. Depending on the size of the prey, the snake needs between a few days and more than a week to digest it.

A green mamba's flexible lower jaw allows it to swallow its meal whole.

Defense

Although snakes are predators, they can also be prey. Many species of snake have developed ways to defend themselves. Poisonous snakes are often brightly colored, warning enemies to stay away. Other snakes scare off predators by lifting their heads up high or thrashing about. When a cobra is angry, a piece of loose skin, called a hood, flares out from behind its head, making it look bigger. Still other snakes can break off a piece of their tail if a **predator** has grabbed it. A new tail grows back.

Snakes also make different sounds as warnings. Some snakes hiss. Rattlesnakes have a rattle on the end of their tails used to scare away any creature that is a threat.

Fun Fact!

A rattlesnake's rattle is made from keratin, the same substance as human fingernails!

A rattlesnake tries to scare off a predator by shaking its rattle.

Snake Families

Snakes, like many reptiles, give off a special scent when it is mating time. Most female snakes lay from six to thirty eggs a few weeks after mating. These hatch in six to twelve weeks. Female snakes do not usually stay with their eggs until they hatch. But some species, such as the king cobra, stay to protect their eggs from predators.

Other snakes, such as rattlesnakes and garter snakes, give birth to live young. Many young snakes do not survive their first year of life. They are eaten by crows, skunks, snapping turtles, other snakes, and other animals.

Fun Fact!

A group of snake eggs is called a clutch.

A baby king cobra hatches. It will face many dangers until it is big enough to defend itself against predators.

Relationship with People

Throughout history, snakes have been both feared and praised by people. The ancient Greek god of healing carried a walking stick with a snake carved on it. Today, this is a symbol of healing. Some people see snakes as a sign of new life since they shed their old skins for new ones. The snake is also a sign in the Chinese Zodiac.

Fun Fact!

In ancient Egypt, the pharaohs wore crowns decorated with Nile cobras.

An ancient Egyptian pharaoh wears a cobra decoration on his crown.

Many people are still afraid of snakes, despite the fact that only a small number of snakes are dangerous. Some people have killed snakes out of fear. But snakes have been killed for other reasons too. In some places, people eat snakes. And their skins are often used to make bags, wallets, belts, and shoes.

However, there are also many people who enjoy snakes. Some are kept as pets in homes, while others are kept in safe environments like zoos and wildlife parks.

Some people think snakes make good pets. But not all snake species are legal to keep as pets.

Endangered Species

There are several species of snakes throughout the world that have become **endangered**, or in danger of dying out. A number of species of sea snakes, constrictors, and vipers are considered endangered worldwide. In the United States, San Francisco garter snakes are endangered.

Many scientists blame this on the fact that the snakes' natural habitats are vanishing. Forests have been cleared and swamps drained to make way for farms and towns, and this leaves the snakes with nowhere to live.

Laws have been passed that prevent endangered snakes from being killed, collected, or sold. Snakes are actually useful to people. They eat rats and mice that destroy farm crops. Snakes are part of nature. It is important that they be here in the future.

Malaysian wildlife authorities rescue reptiles that were being smuggled out of the country.

Stay Safe Around Snakes

Summer has been called "snake season" because many snakes enjoy the warm weather. Snakes may be out more, but so are people. It's best to remember that snakes really don't want anything to do with humans. However, if you are out hiking or camping, you may come across a snake. You may even see a snake in your backyard. Here are a few rules to follow to stay safe:

- While outdoors, do not leave known trails or reach into rock piles, bushes, or logs.

- If you see a snake, don't try to chase it or pick it up. Many snakes only attack when they feel threatened.

- If you're going into an area where you know there are snakes, wear boots that cover the ankle. Doing this could stop about 25 percent of snakebites.

- If you're camping, be sure and check your boots in the morning before you put them on. Snakes like dark places to sleep, just like you do.

- If you do get bit, have an adult take you to the hospital immediately.

- Never keep a wild snake as a pet.

Learn More

Books

Bishop, Nic. *Snakes*. New York: Scholastic, Inc., 2012.

Discovery Channel. *Discovery Snakeopedia*. Des Moines, Iowa: Time Home Entertainment Books, 2014.

Munro, Roxie. *Slithery Snakes*. Las Vegas: Amazon Children's Publishing, 2013.

Woodward, John. *Everything You Need to Know About Snakes and Other Scaly Reptiles*. New York: DK Smithsonian, 2013.

Web Sites

animals.sandiegozoo.org/animals/snake
Read more about snakes and their habits.

kids.nationalgeographic.com/animals/burmese-python/
Learn about the Burmese Python.

discoverykids.com/articles/slitherin-snakes/
View cool photos of snakes.

Index

Published in 2016 by Enslow Publishing, LLC.
101 West 23rd Street, Suite 240, New York, NY 10011

Library of Congress Cataloging-in-Publication Data
  O'Shaughnessy, Ruth, author.
  Snakes after dark / Ruth O'Shaughnessy.
    pages cm. — (Animals of the night)
  Summary: "Discusses snakes, their behavior, and their
    environment"—Provided by publisher.
  Audience: Ages 8+
  Audience: Grades 4 to 6.
  Includes bibliographical references and index.
  ISBN 978-0-7660-6768-4 (library binding)
  ISBN 978-0-7660-6766-0 (pbk.)
  ISBN 978-0-7660-6767-7 (6-pack)
  1. Snakes—Juvenile literature. 2. Nocturnal animals—Juvenile
    literature. 3. Animal behavior—Juvenile literature. I. Title.
  QL666.O69O84 2016
  597.96—dc23
                      2015009971

Printed in the United States of America

To Our Readers: We have done our best to make sure all Web site addresses in this book were active and appropriate when we went to press. However, the author and the publisher have no control over and assume no liability for the material available on those Web sites or on any Web sites they may link to. Any comments or suggestions can be sent by e-mail to customerservice@enslow.com.

Portions of this book originally appeared in the book *Big Snakes: Hunters of the Night*.

Photo Credits: AFP/Getty Images, p. 29; Brad Wilson/The Image Bank/Getty Images, p. 5; Christian Meermann/Moment Open/Getty Images (green snake), p. 1; De Agostini/S. Vannini/De Agostini Picture Library/Getty images, p. 25; George Grall/National Geographic/Getty Images p. 13; Henry Cook/Moment/Getty Images, p. 7; John Cancalosi/Photolibrary/Getty Images, p. 11; kimberrywood/Digital Vision Vectors/Getty Images (green moon dingbats); Martin Cohen Wild About Australia/Lonely Planet Images/Getty Images, p. 17; narvikk/E+/Getty Images (starry background); Photo Researchers/Science Source/Getty Images, p. 9; R. Andrew Odum/Photolibrary/Getty, p. 15; Rebecca Abell/Shutterstock.com, p. 27; Ryan M. Bolton/Shutterstock.com, p. 21; samxmeg/E+/Getty Images (moon folios and series logo); suebg1 photography/Moment/Getty Images, p. 3; The Sydney Morning Herald/ Fairfax Media/Getty Images, p. 23; Visuals Unlimited, Inc./Robert Pickett/Getty Images, p. 19.

Cover Credits: Christian Meermann/Moment Open/Getty Images (green snake); narvikk/E+/Getty Images (starry background); kimberrywood/Digital Vision Vectors/Getty Images (green moon dingbat); samxmeg/E+/Getty Images (moon).